John Colman Rashleigh

**The Case of the People of England**

John Colman Rashleigh

**The Case of the People of England**

ISBN/EAN: 9783337797102

Printed in Europe, USA, Canada, Australia, Japan

Cover: Foto ©Suzi / pixelio.de

More available books at **www.hansebooks.com**

# THE CASE

OF THE

# PEOPLE OF ENGLAND,

ADDRESSED TO THE

" LIVES AND FORTUNE MEN,"

BOTH IN AND OUT OF

## The Houſe of Commons;

*As a Ground for National Thankſgiving!*

By one of the 80,000 incorrigible Jacobins.

---

Eſpecially give us Grace not to be elated with Proſperity.
*Form of Prayer and Thankſgiving.*

Here—take an Inventory of all I have;
To the laſt Penny 'tis the King's!   *Shakeſpeare.*

---

LONDON:

PRINTED FOR R. H. WESTLEY, NO. 201, STRAND.

MDCCXCVIII.

TO THE

## LIVES AND FORTUNE MEN.

---

GENTLEMEN,

THE people of England have been commanded by a royal proclamation, to set apart a day from the ordinary business and pursuits of life, to perform an act of national humiliation and thanksgiving, to Almighty God, for the victories and success with which he has crowned the arms of this country. The propriety of such an act ought to be as clear as the act itself is awful. For the suspension of the industry of the city of London for a single day, is of such immense consequence to a commercial community, that it can only be justified by strong and urgent reasons. But its industry is suspended in the present instance, to celebrate a festival of gratitude to the Giver of all good things; of whom, we are amongst other things commanded to pray, *that we should not be elevated by Success*. No prayer can be more proper;—but in the mean time permit me to ask you, Gentlemen,

Gentlemen, whether such a prayer is at the present moment necessary? And whether we are quite correct in celebrating a festival of success and victory.

At least I fear that this proclamation is not quite in unison with the public feeling. The people of this country do not want much religious discipline to subdue their arrogance or exultation: their wonder, or rather their indignation, is excited, when they hear this language of triumph held by the very men who have so lately called on them, for such immense and cruel sacrifices, not to support the glory, but to preserve the existence of the country. The pomp and splendour of a public spectacle is a sorry compensation to them and their starving families—the delight of such a scene is lost in the bitter recollection of the means, by which its expence must be defrayed. For the procession to St. Paul's forms a wretched contrast to the debates and votes of the committee of supply.

Indeed the conduct of the government and propertied orders of the community, is not very consistent with prudence and common sense—It is not a happy comment on their own declarations, nor a good pledge of their sincerity. The generous and confiding people entered into this war because you bade them do so. It was *your* interest that they should fight—for it has been a war, in defence of order and property—It has been a war therefore, almost exclusively *your own*. What they have suffered and sacrificed

crificed in your defence, you ought to know, if you have taken care, that they have not been plundered and cheated gratuitoufly; and there is no fuffering and facrifice that you called on them to make, which they have not readily complied with. You ftill told them that all would end well. The end it is true is not yet come. But as you have now in the fame breath called on them for help, and commanded them to celebrate good fortune, they have a right to know of you, (and depend upon it they will one day know) how thefe apparent contradictions can be reconciled; why they are to undergo frefh fufferings, and what advantages they have gained from thofe that are paft.

And but that you have told us, and that you have the high authority of his Majefty for your opinion, that it was expedient to offer thankfgiving for fuccefs; it would not be a very exaggerated ftatement of our prefent fituation, to fum it up in one comprehenfive term—Ruin. For to what a condition is the country reduced by the war? What a contraft is the year 1792 to the year 1797.—From profperity we have paffed to bankruptcy.—From vain-glory to defpair! This tranfition of events is as fingular, as the tafk of detailing them is difgufting! But the tranfition of public feeling, when its grounds are confidered, is both natural and juft. Thofe who are guilty of intemperance in one extreme will be guilty of it in the other:—this is true of nations as well as individuals.

You

You who were so clamorous for war because confident of success, call in a little honest memory to assist you, in recollecting your motives and language in the year 1792. Do you believe, that had France and England held their present relative situations in the year 1792, that your moral sensibilities would have been as irritable against atheists and jacobins, or that you would have been as eager to assert the cause of order and religion, as when the alluring bait of national aggrandizement, and commercial gain, tempted your ambitious lusts, and made you first adopt as a pretext for war, the Anarchy of France; and then delude yourselves into a belief that you had never engaged for any other object than that holy and righteous cause? No. A commercial nation never yet had so much generous Quixotism about its character. I remember well the speculations that were indulged in, weak and wicked as they were: I remember the vaunting presumption that led you to imagine that the declining commerce, ruined manufactures, and unprotected colonies of France, would be an easy prey to your superior resources. Commercial men are said to take unfair advantages of each other in private life: commercial nations will do the same: though it is questionable whether dishonesty is good policy in either case.

But let your hopes of 1792 have been what they may, in 1797 they are at least disappointed. The war, whether it was begun for aggrandizement or glory

glory, is now continued for existence. *We affect therefore to celebrate the Victory, when we ought to be content to survive the struggle.* In France we no longer behold a people suing for peace, divided amongst themselves, agitated by fierce and bloody factions, with civil war in her heart and a powerful confederacy on her frontier: we do not now behold a land covered with blood and mourning, nor her most eminent citizens dragged in crouds to the scaffolds of her revolutionary tyrants!—Nor does the minister of this country (as then he did) hold in one hand the balance of European fate, whilst with the other, like the Argantes of Tasso, from the folds of his robe, he scattered death and war and famine over a devoted world. The lowly head has been raised, and the proud laid low. We, who at first came forward full of resources and with all Europe for our ally, now remain single and exhausted, to conclude the contest. Whilst with the whole principle of her strength yet entire, France has detached, either by force or persuasion, almost every power of Europe from our cause, and attached them to her own.— Well may the people ask the reason of your rejoicing at such a prospect—well may they droop. For would it not be to reason in an inverted order, if we were able to accomplish that in a state of weakness which we were unable to perform in a state of strength. I say not this to dishearten the people—At the present crisis he would be an enemy to his country that would do so. But it is not therefore necessary to *delude* them; they have been already too long and often the victims of delusion, or the country would at this instant have reposed on the bosom of Peace. It is to prevent a continuation of that delusion that I now write; unless this is effected, I am as sure as I am that I exist, that the country is ruined. You may by a military goverment extort requisitions; you may proclaim fasts and celebrate victories; and the people may starve in silence, whilst you triumph with impunity. But, you will not by these means ward off the danger which you know threatens you, nor render it less terrible because its extent is disguised and its arrival protracted. You must ascend to the origin of the evil, if it is to be removed. All palliatives, all expedients are worse than insufficient in such a state of affairs as the present. Either persevere in your system, or resolve to adopt a new one. And do so, whilst yet it is permitted you to make a choice: If you will do this, honestly and sincerely, I trust that there is yet left to the cause of England, all that ought ever to have made her confident;—the justice of self-defence.

For however I reprobate that sentiment of exultation in which I think the English people indulged at the beginning of the war; still it is the excess, or rather abuse, of a generous feeling.—But despair can never be consistent with the dignity of a great people. Political inactivity can never be justified; whilst the
common

common-wealth exifts, it fhould never be defpaired of. The coward only lies down and dies, the brave man, even in the midft of adverfe and finking fortunes, can find wherewithal to confole and even adorn his fall. I do not therefore for one credit the oppofition to the full extent of their declared feceffion. I ftill think it is but a political manœuvre; but whether it is or is not, of this I am fure, that in times like thefe to indulge in defpair is difgraceful, but to record it is a crime—he furely will be efteemed by enlightened and impartial hiftory as the wifer and better example, who buries in the diftrefs of his country all fenfe of private wrong, than he who cherifhing a peevifh refentment at her ingratitude, undoes at the fame time his country and his own glory. Therefore I hope and truft that the people do not defpair—languid they have hitherto been, but they have been fo for want of a caufe to awaken their energies; but give them a caufe, " and they will aroufe as a giant from fleep, or a " ftrong man refrefhed by wine."

What France has been, I truft England can be. If peace was fought in the fpirit of fincerity, I fhould commend the man who refufed to compromife the interefts of his country for an ignominious repofe. What I thought of the fpeculations of the allied powers, that think I now of the councils of France; they are the dreams of a diftempered ambition: for, as when her frontier was invaded by a foe that thought to

B 2 make

make her a prey, through her weakness, every heart beat thick with indignation, and every arm was lifted up to assert the cause of liberty and man; so ought she to recollect that in this country the same causes will produce the same effects; every order and class of men will, I hope, combine their efforts with a common and equal zeal to preserve their independence, and to prevent our being what we never yet have been, a conquered nation. We should not, I hope, be conquered even into liberty. For I hold that nation to be unworthy, if not incapable of freedom, which cannot free herself. But France has, on this score, surely held out no very extraordinary temptations. I think that Englishmen will do well to remember the fate of Holland, of Venice, and the Cis-Rhenane republic before she imitates their example.—But we can neither think rightly nor act justly without full and free enquiry. We must ascend to the fountain head, or our energy will avail us little. Let us remember that it is of necessity impossible for men to reason justly from wrong premises; and as we act in conformity to our opinions, we must ascend at once to first causes and principles, or we had better rest where we are. Now with respect to the present war, it is so obviously and closely connected with the French revolution, that it is impossible to discuss the one without alluding to the other. I shall not enter into an analysis of its causes; all that I know of it is, its effects. They were in France a radical change in

the

the social system; in other countries an agitation of public sentiment, producing great, and in some instances alarming dissensions, as that event corresponded to the hopes or fears of men. In this country there appeared from the first three leading parties: those who conceiving that it had substantiated the power of a political sect and doctrine, which had long been rising in France, and which had a tendency to subvert the whole principle of European society, contemplated the overthrow of the antient regimen in France with terror, and saw only in the new order of things, a monster, against which the whole force and energy of existing society should be instantly exerted. They conceived that it was an absurd and dangerous delay, to wait for the formality of *overt* acts of aggression, from a system, which of itself was a grand *overt* act against all contrary modes of established authority and usage. They conceived, that however the leaders of the rising sect might temporize, yet there was an hostility inherent in their system, which must at some time or other manifest itself against the opposite one, and that its leaders were impressed with the persuasion, that both systems could not co-exist. They therefore were desirous of instantly opposing it by declared and open warfare, because it was as yet weak, as being in a state of embryo and experiment, whilst the regular governments, whose interest it was to crush it, were

entire

entire and mature. This is the party of the late Mr. Burke.

Opposed to these, if not in the other extreme, yet certainly *magno intervallo* stood the party of Mr. Fox, and those who, however they differed on subordinate points of speculation, have acted and thought with him. They beheld in the French revolution the triumph of Liberty over despotism, of reason over error, of mankind over their oppressors. They indeed knew that a free goverment must give to France a power greater than she had ever possessed under her despotism. But although they believed that the continent of Europe might be materially affected by so great a change, and that it would be the means sooner or later of reversing the whole scheme of its civil regimen; yet in this prospect they saw nothing but matter of triumph and exultation to Britons; certainly nothing for which the reflecting mind must not have been long prepared by the events of the last and the preceding century.

The intrepidity of thought that had effected a reformation in religion, had spread itself to civil government. The Italian republics, the Hanseatic league, the emancipation of the people of Holland, the commonwealth of England, the revolution of 1688, and lastly the independence of America, were a series of revolutions connected by a chain of necessary causes. They were only *different Æras in the History of the same Principle*, viz. the gradual preva-

lence

lence of Freedom over Tyranny. The French revolution could not therefore be to them a matter of surprize, for as from each of the preceding events fresh discoveries and bolder experiments had been made in political science, so all these examples served to be to France, a basis on which wider notions of polity and more enlarged conceptions of human nature might erect the fabric of social institution. Nor could they consider the change which had taken place in France as a matter of alarm to this country— they rather foresaw in it the happiest political consequences: much of that national hostility, which had been the cause of so many wars between the two countries, had not been so much owing to a *competition in politics*, as to great and essential *differences of opinion*. The intolerance of a blind and ferocious bigotry, joined to the spirit of a despotic government, were in France exasperated against a contrary mode of Faith, and a more liberal system of political relations. That furious zeal which had oppressed the Hugonots, which had opposed the reformation, which had propagated its faith by fire and sword, was united in the councils of Louis XIV. with an insatiable thirst of conquest and glory. In England that faith had been expelled, the maxims and form of despotism exploded; and her religious and civil liberties consolidated by the revolution of 1688. Hence the wars which arose between her and France, (although power was the ostensible, as well as a component

ponent caufe) yet they were more or lefs a conflict and war of opinions: until therefore one or other of the oppofite fyftems was deftroyed, there appeared but little probability of fincere or lafting repofe. But *ceſſante cauſá ceſſat effectus*, the overthrow of the French government and its eftablifhed religion feemed to Mr. Fox's party to have overthrown alfo the principle of animofity between the two nations. And the erection of a free government in France, as it gave the people of the two countries a fympathy of habits, interefts, and fentiments, opened not only a profpect of conciliation and repofe, but of ftrict amity and cordial friendfhip and union.

Intermediate between thefe was the party of Mr. Pitt, or rather the great body of the Englifh public who fupported his adminiftration. In fome refpects they differed and in fome agreed with each of the others. As it is of importance to a clear conception of the real defigns of the miniftry in entering into the prefent war, that their general opinion of the French revolution fhould be afcertained; I have taken pains to eftablifh my ftatement of it by fuch documents and evidence as it has been in my power to collect: thefe I cannot here bring forward, as a full expofition of their contents is incompatible with the fize of a pamphlet. The great body of the people, who never look to remote confequences, and who judge of events by their immediate effects, expreffed a general and honeft joy at the firft overthrow

of

of the despotism of France, because they conceived that the people must be happy when they were free. But this was no more than a vulgar prejudice, which did not contemplate the tendency of such a change with respect to France or Europe. Like every opinion of the people it was liable to rapid and capricious fluctuations, as that event unfolded itself in consequences, which the common apprehension of mankind had been incapable of foreseeing. Therefore as they continued to judge by appearances, their favor or disfavor succeeded each other, as the revolution wore an aspect favorable or unfavorable to their national prejudices. For instance, I believe the joy at the emancipation of the French was general, until in establishing their freedom they deviated from the mode of English liberty. When they abolished hereditary distinctions, and rejected the plan of a divided legislature, the English public no longer respected in its detail the liberty it had applauded in its principle. But this amounted to no more than speculative dislike, a dislike natural to the mind of man whilst it is governed by passions and sympathies. But the government of England was a distinct body from the public; they had never from the first cordially rejoiced at the freedom of the French; they observed indeed a cold and rigid silence as to their internal affairs, although I believe that in the abstract they disliked the principle of the revolution, because its genius was adverse to the system of their own power, the former being

founded

founded on democratic, the latter on ariftocratic and propertied interefts. But I conceive that they thought interference inexpedient for two reafons: 1ft. That the temper of this People, and the abfence of the neceffity which had produced a change in France, rendered the influence of French principles flight and feeble, and confequently did not menace their power with an alarming danger. And the other, by far the moft important, (fince I conceive that the fpirit of this principle has been the mafter policy of the war) is a reafon that was admirably adapted to the half informed part of a commercial public: viz. the effects which the revolution was likely to have on the *Power of France*, particularly on her commerce, her manufactures, and her finances; the decline of which, as they were objects of rivalry between her and England, would proportionably give the latter an afcendancy in the fcale of nations. I fhall endeavour to prove hereafter, that this policy, as it at firft difpofed the miniftry to be neutral, fo it afterwards from change of circumftances induced them to go to war. In fhort, that their *one and only object has been foreign and domeftic Power*.

I have ftated the different principles of thefe parties, to prove the refpective claims of each to found political calculation, and I think that if there is a truth fufceptible of demonftration it is, that from the views, the reafoning, and the conduct of the prefent minifter, he has proved himfelf not only

to

to have been unequal to the exigency of so important an occasion: but that he is as incapable of great political design, as of ingenious and original resource: of the merit of his policy we may judge, by comparing it with the opinions of the other parties, illustrated as they have been by the progress of the French revolution and the war. And on the measures which he has adopted to attain his ends, a little attention to the history of events, and their effects, will enable us to determine. And let it be remembered that if he is convicted of errors in judgment, in the course of this review, he has not the same excuse to plead (miserable as it must be in public men, if it was pleaded at all) which sometimes extenuates such cases. For inasmuch as both friends and enemies again and again, in public and in private, pointed out to him the fallacy of his calculations, and the ruinous tendency of his measures, he has added the guilt of obstinacy to ignorance, an obstinacy that united with delusion, has reduced the country to a state, from which, it is a doubt, whether the wisdom or virtue of any man, will be able to redeem it.

To support this opinion, viz. that power was his object; and that the same policy which induced him to be neutral at one time, rendered him at another actively hostile, I shall take two grounds; the first rests on the external evidence, which the course of events, and the conduct of the minister before and after the war, afford;—the second on the internal evidence, that is derived from the inconsistency of his declarations, in his statements of the objects of the war; as well as the incongruity of his ends and means.

Now on the first head, viz. the external evidence of the question, the minister of this country was relieved from all apprehension of views of aggrandizement in France previous to the war; because from her state in 1789, she was incapable, and had declared herself to be unwilling to attempt them. She had by a solemn decree, renounced the system of conquest, nay had expressed doubts (Mr. Pitt perhaps thought them fanatical) whether she could justly retain her colonial possessions. In all the debates of her legislature on the external interests of the state, they not only incidentally recognized the absolute necessity of peace to the completion of their work, but particularly expressed an ardent desire to confirm and strengthen the bands of friendship and amity between the two countries. From necessity, as well as inclination, this country had therefore nothing to fear from France.

But in the light of policy, every thing might be hoped for from her internal state; and the effects which her revolution had produced on her finances. Their re-establishment formed the chief labour of her new legislature. " The finances alone, demand " perhaps, for half a century, our legislative labours,"

said

said Mirabeau, in the debate on the *Veto*; and the declaration of Mirabeau was followed up by the constant attention of the assembly. In the mean time, their opulence, as a trading and manufacturing country rapidly declined: to this their own confessions and measures bore invariable testimony; whilst this country had, in a few years, exhibited a picture of commercial resuscitation, unparalelled in the history of the world. Whilst France was left to herself, the re-establishment of her credit appeared to be a more and more difficult task: for on what does the finance or public credit of a country depend? certainly on the stability of its government; since public credit is nothing more than a belief, that property is safe under the protective influence of the government: but the convulsion which the new order of things occasioned, the intrigues and changes of parties, and the dread of a counter revolution, continued to check the efforts of the assembly to accomplish this end; and in the mean time England was enabled from the influence of her pacific system, to profit daily by that derangement.

Again, as to domestic concerns, I do not conceive the minister had reason for alarm, nor did he entertain any, lest serious effects should be produced by French principles in this country; because in the first first place, the people *were loyal, and attached to the constitution, and did not suffer the evils which have always been necessary to produce a revolution.* In the next place, Mr. Pitt did not feel this alarm, since the

the opinions which had caused it had not grown up, or been discovered on a sudden. They existed to full the same extent, as to the number and weight of their advocates, in the years 1790—91, as in 1792—93. Societies were established in England, they corresponded with the affiliated clubs at Paris; the press teemed with their publications, yet all these facts were notorious to ministers, and still they were suffered to pass nearly unnoticed. Therefore I conclude, *that there was neither reason for alarm, nor that alarm did exist in the mind of Mr. Pitt, on account of revolutionary doctrines:* for if there did, in what a predicament does he stand? Either he knew of the growth of these societies, or he did not. If he did know of them, and they were of so dangerous a nature as to become afterwards a just cause of war, or at least of social agitation and alarm, the public owes but little to the providence or virtue of a minister, who did not crush the evil in its beginning. And inasmuch as the end of laws and punishments is to prevent crimes, why did he not interfere before these treasons had risen to so alarming an height, as to require a sacrifice from the subject of the bulwark of his civil liberty, the *Habeas Corpus* act: why did he not interfere before the lives of men (whether deceived or deceiving, is of no consequence) were brought into imminent peril? If he knew of such proceedings, and did not check them, he is convicted of a criminal neglect of the public weal, and a wicked abuse of his
authority.

authority. If he did not know of their exiſtence, what credit does he deſerve for vigilance, when he was ignorant of facts that were notorious to every other man in the country.

I believe therefore that his power was ſafe, and that he believed it to be ſafe from the diſorganizing tendency of French principles, previous to the year 1792. But it was eſſentially neceſſary to the continuance of his domeſtic power to remain neutral, ſince whatever diſguſt had been excited in the people at large againſt the proceedings of the convention: and though Mr. Burke had long raiſed his cry for the cruſade; yet war was too hazardous an experiment to be undertaken by a miniſter at ſuch riſks, and under ſo equivocal a ſtate of the public ſentiment. Beſides, all that could be hoped for from the overthrow of French principles, was hoped for from the confederacy of Auſtria and Pruſſia. The expence and odium of a war could be avoided, whilſt all its benefits would be reaped gratuitouſly by the Engliſh miniſter.

Thus much for neutrality being conſiſtent with foreign and domeſtic power, previous to the year 1792.—It remains to be ſhewn why war was expedient on the ſame ground, ſubſequent to that period.

Men of the *Gironde* and of the Mountain, whatever may have been your crimes as moral agents, as republicans you ſaved France. You gave to her revolution

volution a new aspect and complexion; from being crippled in her energies, by the inefficient and pacific "*democracié royale*" of 1789, she had assumed "the" "port" and attributes of a military republic! She no longer renounced former acquisitions, she made new conquests; she no longer deprecated the anger and jealousy of other governments, in the language of low-voiced and puling eloquence; she bade defiance to all open and secret enemies, and reared against the whole antient world, the banner of her revolution. Instead of debating on the independence of a savage horde, or a distant island, she had formally annexed Savoy and Nice to her republic. Instead of hunting for expedients and palliatives of finance amongst the musty records and tame precedents of the funding system, she seised on the collective capital of the country, a project the most daring and gigantic, in its conception, that is recorded in the annals of revolution. Instead of being a prey to foreign plunderers, she had become an armed nation.

As before she had contented herself with discussing political theories with the calmness of a school of philosophers, so now she made converts by the roar of cannon, and the point of the bayonet. By these means she had broken through the balance of power, violated all rules of finance, and consequently frustrated all calculations built on her former proceedings, and converted that which was before a *moral cause* into a *political instrument*. Her empire no longer
rested

rested on opinion alone; it was a mixed principle of power and sentiment, the one upholding and spreading the other.

I think then that *if the attainment of power was the minister's policy*, this change in the state of Europe, rendered a change in his system necessary. France could no longer be left to herself; she could no longer be trusted to the Prussian and Austrian confederacy;—her finances must now die a *violent* not a *natural* death; her power be crushed at once, before it became too strong for Europe. But do not the language and the conduct of ministers throughout the war tally with this notion? Look at their calculations on finance, on the depreciation of the assignats; look at their comparative statements of the Power of Great Britain and France; look at the language held by Mr. Dundas on the annexation of Corsica to the crown of England; on the capture of the Cape of Good Hope; on the discussion of the principle of compensation, in the debates on the late negociation for peace; look at *those negociations themselves*; and at the tenor of their measures during the war. Wherever other objects have been concerned, their language has been equivocal, their views indistinct, and the execution of their plans feeble and inefficient. Yet how vigorous and unremitting have been their efforts, how immense their expence of blood and treasure, when directed to the object of power. Let the West Indian expeditions

tions and our immense naval armaments speak to this point. And then let it be decided, whether from the testimony of such facts it is to be believed, that they were in earnest as to the other objects of the war. Whether such vigour and decision on one hand, and such confusion and delay on the other, can consist in the same characters. But how stands the case from the event of the war? They have succeeded in the temporary attainment of one object, viz. the possession of the colonies, and the ruin of the trade of France; and all the others are not only not attained, but are despaired of, and relinquished by ministers themselves.

If we look at home, we shall find not only, that subsequent to the year 1792, war was consistent with this policy; but that in fact, power the most unbounded has been acquired and confirmed to Mr. Pitt by that event.

The cry for war was not now uttered by a few feeble voices. The success of French arms and principles had alarmed the political and commercial fears of the whole English public. The walls of the House of Commons rang with anathemas against the conduct of the French, and their proselytizing spirit. At the head of these, stood those members of the whig party, who differing from all their old political connexions presented to Mr. Pitt the opportunity of a coalition, which would for ever secure the system of his domestic power. What was the result; that party became

December 13th, 1792.
The King's speech has the following passage.

I have carefully observed a strict neutrality in the present war on the continent, and have uniformly abstained from any interference in the internal affairs of France.

June 17th, 1793.
Mr. Pitt says:

There was nothing in any communication from the throne by which he should feel himself precluded from advising his Majesty to interfere in the internal affairs of France, if an opportunity should occur of converting that interference into the means of obtaining the objects of the war.

July 10th, 1794.
He says as before.
" An object from which he
" never would depart, &c."

June 17th, 1793.
He says:

He did not maintain that we were to persist in an impolitic war, merely because we had right on our side.

April 25th, 1793.
Mr. Pitt says:

That this war was *neither begun nor carried on for the purpose of interfering in the internal polity of France, or, of establishing in that country any form of government whatever, an object, therefore, the attainment of which, was not essential to the termination of the war.*

June 17th, 1793.
He says:

" He had formerly said, that
" he did not consider any
" form of government which
" the French might attempt to
" establish as a just ground of
" war."—" He said so still."

July 10th, 1794.
Mr. Pitt says:

The avowed object of the war was none of those which had been ascribed to ministers, it was simply this: *the destruction of the system of Jacobinism in France. This object was neither to be heightened by new grounds of success, nor relinquished from any temporary failure in the means of its attainment, and was one from which he would never depart, as absolutely necessary to the security and preservation of this country and its allies.*

January 26th, 1795.
He moves an amendment to Mr. Grey's motion for peace.

Whenever a reasonable expectation of obtaining peace presented itself, they relied with the utmost confidence on his Majesty, that he would apply the resources of the country to the attainment of so desirable an object, with any government in France, *IF it should appear capable* of maintaining the accustomed relations of peace and amity.

came united to his interests; and the remaining opposition too feeble to form an administration. Nor can the Duke of Portland and his party now recede: they must consent to continue attached to Mr. Pitt and his fortunes, or cease to exist as political characters in this country.

*Facilis descensus Averni;*
*Sed revocare gradum superasque evadere ad auras,*
*Hoc opus, hic labor!*

So much for the external evidence of the question.
The internal evidence is to be collected
1st. From the inconsistency of the minister in his statements of the objects of the war.
And 2ndly, from the inconveniency of the measures pursued to the ends proposed.

To prove his Inconsistency with himself, I submit the opposite Extracts from the Debates of Parliament.

Now as to the second point: viz. the inconveniency of the measures pursued, to the ends proposed,
I shall consider it under two heads:
1st. With respect to our domestic transactions.
2dly. As to objects of foreign policy and interest.

Now what is the history of our domestic transactions as they relate to the war?
First, whilst it was impending, his Majesty in his speech of the 13th of December, 1792, declared;

*That*

" *That he had observed a strict neutrality in the present
" war on the continent, and had uniformly abstained
" from any interference in the internal affairs of France.*
" But it was impossible for him to see without the
" most serious uneasiness the strong and encreasing
" indications which have appeared, there, of an
" intention to excite disturbances in other countries;
" to disregard the rights of neutral nations, &c.
" Under all these circumstances he had thought it
" right to take steps for making some augmentation
" of his military force, &c.—being persuaded that
" these exertions were necessary, &c. to render a
" firm and temperate conduct *effectual for preserving*
" *the blessings of peace.*

" Nothing *would be neglected on his part* that can
" contribute to that important object consistently
" with the honor of this country, &c.

To this speech an address was returned echoing and approving it. Now what is it's import, and to what did the government stand pledged? You thereby declared it to be true, that you had observed a neutrality in the war, and that you had abstained from any interference in the internal affairs of France. And by having done so *carefully*, you acknowledged that it was right to have done so. With what state had you observed neutrality and abstained from interference? with what state, did you promise to omit no means consistent with your honour, to preserve the blessings of peace?—With a
republic

republic, without a conftitution, and in a ftate of revolution.

If then it was right to be neutral and to avoid interference, it could not be alfo right to go to war and interfere, on account of the internal affairs of that country. If peace was defirable, and you wifhed to maintain its bleffings, and if it was likely to be interrupted by *particular circumftances*, viz. views of aggrandizement, attempts to excite difcontent, &c. if you omitted no means to obtain this end, you would endeavour to remove thofe circumftances; and when they were removed, would reftore things to the original footing of peace.

And you yourfelves recognized this doctrine; you declared in the debate of the houfe, that it was not the *government* of France you armed againft, but certain indications of hoftility which it had betrayed by particular acts, and declarations. Mr. Dundas, a minifter, laid down exprefsly as the grounds of war, the decree of the 19th of November, the views of aggrandizement entertained by the French, and their violation of treaties and the rights of neutral nations. Therefore thefe grounds are the *overt* acts of the goverment, and not it's *principle*, for with that his Majefty declined to " interfere," and expreffed a defire to continue at peace.

This diftinction rendered the prefent war on its original grounds, analagous in principle to all former wars that had taken place between this country and France.

You

You declared hostilities against Louis XIV. not because he was a tyrant and a catholic, but because his schemes of universal monarchy, and his attempt to place the Pretender on the English throne, and to subvert the protestant religion, were *acts of aggression:* The former similar to the conquest of the Netherlands, &c. the latter to the decree of the 19th of November: but when those *acts of aggression* were done away, you made peace with the government and religion of France. So in this case, as you had thought it right to remain for so long a time neutral, and to avoid interference; you therefore shewed that it was not with the *existence* of republicanism or jacobinism, that you went to war. It was on account of it's *acts* that you thought it necessary to arm *to prevent the necessity of absolute hostilities.* I therefore infer from your former neutrality, from your avowed desire of peace, and the alledged grounds of impending hostility, that you were bound by your own declarations *to seek the best means* of removing them, and when removed, to restore things to their former state.

Now what means can be taken by nations in the case of *impending* hostilities? Are there any other pointed out, either by the law of nations or common sense, than negotiation? let me ask the ministers of England, whether or no, they negotiated with France in a spirit of sincerity to "preserve the blessings of peace?" If you were desirous of obtaining that object, you must allow that it was your duty to

use

use every means of conciliation with the oppofite party, confiftent with your own dignity. If in him you had met with fymptoms of a favourable difpofition, you would encourage and ftrengthen the propenfity, and evince by all means, a fpirit ready to meet pacific and healing overtures.

In private life, if you apprehended a quarrel with your neighbour, with whom you ftill wifhed to be on good terms, you would avoid as much as poffible occafions of giving frefh difguft ; and on the contrary embrace opportunities for the renewal of good underftanding. You would not conceive it to be a very efficacious method, to prevent hatred, to tell your neighbour to his face, that you had a defire to continue friends, and at the fame time blacken his character with others, on all poffible and public occafions, defigning that he fhould hear of it again : you would not, when he fent one of his family to you to make up exifting differences, treat that agent with ftudied contempt, and deny his authority to act, becaufe fome part of your neighbour's family had fuffered in a domeftic difpute, in which you had before declared you would have no concern? You would not, when at length you condefcended to talk to this agent, on the fubject of reconciliation, take care that he and your neighbour fhould know, that, at that very time you were inftigating the neighbourhood againft them, on account of the abovementioned domeftic difpute? Is it reafonable to fuppofe pose that such conduct could conciliate? Yet thus you acted in your endeavour to preserve peace with your neighbour the French republic.

For did you not take every opportunity of abusing the government and governors of France? Did you not attribute your domestic discontents to their direct agency? Was not an indecent triumph expressed by you at the first successes of the Duke of Brunswick, although you were then neutral and at peace? Was it consistent with views of peace to deny an authority, by which only negotiation could take place; and to send out of the kingdom with insult, the only man who could negotiate? Was it consistent with a pacific intention, to declare with Mr. Pitt, on the 1st of February, " that you were " not at war with France," and yet request of the States General, by Lord Auckland, on the 25th of January, " that they would take the most efficacious " measures to prevent the persons who might render " themselves guilty of so atrocious a crime *, from " finding any asylum in their respective dominions." " Some of these detested regicides were already in a " situation, *in which they may be subjected to the sword* " *of the law?*" Yet these detested regicides were the men with whom you professed a desire of preserving peace.

It is in vain to say you were not parties to this

---

\* The King's death.

tranfaction:

transaction: you became *accessaries after the fact*, by not impeaching the minister who dared to hold such language in the name of his nation; but this you refused to do: and by justifying the doer, you approved of the deed.

But were not these pretended or alledged grounds of war removed, first, even by the scandalous negotiation which you carried on with M. Chauvelin; and if not then, at all events, at a subsequent period of the war?

In note No. 6, which he delivered to Lord Grenville, the interference alluded to by the King's proclamation is most solemnly renounced by M. Chauvelin, in the name of his nation.

In note No. 13, there are these passages relative to the specific causes of disagreement. First, as to the decree of the 19th of November, he says, "The "National Convention never meant that the French "republic should favour insurrections, should espouse "the quarrels of a few seditious persons; or in a "word, should endeavour to excite disturbances in "any neutral or friendly power whatever. Such an "idea would be rejected by all the French. It "cannot be imputed to the National Convention "without doing it injustice. *This decree then is ap-* "*plicable only to those people, who after having ac-* "*quired their liberty by conquest, may have demanded* "*the fraternity, the assistance of the republic, by the* "*solemn and unequivocal expression of the general will.*"

E            This

This explanation was, however, deemed unsatisfactory. The Executive Council then speaks itself, to remove the misunderstanding. "We have said, and
"we desire to repeat it, that the decree of the 19th
"of November could not have any application, un-
"less to the *single case*, in which the *general will* of a
"nation clearly and unequivocally expressed, should
"call the French nation to its assistance and frater-
"nity. Sedition can certainly never be construed
"into *the general will*. These two ideas mutually
"repel each other, since a sedition is not, and can-
"not be any other than the movement of a small
"number against the nation at large; and this move-
"ment would cease to be seditious, provided all the
"members of a society should at once rise, either to
"correct their government, or to change it *in toto*,
"or for any other object."

Now is or is not this distinction conclusive on the case of England, as it was described by Mr. Pitt himself. "As to the productions of another country,
"he was sure they would not be relished, nor did he
"believe they could have existence, except by the
"management *of a few factious persons; the truth was,*
"*these principles did not agree with ours; their natural*
"*origin was not here, nor was there any thing to be*
"*feared from them.*" Why then if the discontents are confined to a *few factious characters*, why quarrel with a decree, which expressly contemplates only the *general will*: whilst it renounces sedition; and

defines

defines sedition to be the movement of a small number against the *nation at large.*

But if this is not sufficient to prove that this ground was removed before the war, did not the Convention afterwards solemnly revoke the decree both in spirit and substance?

As to the infringement of the rights of our allies, in note No. 13, it is said, "That France ought "and will respect not only the independence of Eng- "land, but even that of those of her allies, with "whom she is not at war. The undersigned has "therefore been charged to declare formally, that "she will not attack Holland, so long as that power, "on its side, confines itself within the bounds of a "strict neutrality."

But at all events, surely these grounds were all done away, when you were possessed of the greatest part of the French frontier, and consequently had stripped her of all her conquests; particularly the Netherlands, and with them the river Scheldt.

So much for your conduct, gentlemen, in endeavouring "to maintain the blessings of peace; and neg- "lecting nothing that could contribute to that desir- "able object."

Now let us look at your conduct, (for by supporting the government, you are a party to its acts) after you entered into the war.

I conceive, gentlemen, that when a man is about to fight, he generally likes to know what he fights for;

E 2        and

and will be heartier in the cause, when he does know, than when he is totally ignorant of the nature of his quarrel. I believe it is pretty much the same with nations. War is too evil and calamitous a principle, to be embraced by mankind, without strong and dire necessity. The sacrifices it exacts require some equivalent: or at least it should be proved to them that they do not throw away the blessings of peace. Therefore you were bound in policy to give the people of this country a specific cause to fight for: to tell them why their purses were emptied and their swords drawn. If so, it follows that the more intelligible the cause is, the more strenuous will be the advocate. Have you acted wisely or honestly in this respect. Both you cannot have done. For if you understood the causes of the war, why did you refuse to make them known to the people? and if you did not, why did you go to war at all?

Now you had the following opportunities given you to specify the objects of the war.

First, Mr. Fox, February 18th, 1793, moved a string of resolutions tending to disclaim particular grounds, as being the causes and objects of the war.—Why did you negative that motion? Next, Mr. Sheridan, April 25th, moved an address on the subject of Lord Auckland's memorial, in order that by disapproving it's contents the house might ascertain " the intent, nature and purpose of the war." This was also negatived.

Mr.

Mr. Fox, June 17th, moved an addreſs for the purpoſe of ſpecifying the preciſe grounds for which we had engaged in, and ſtill continued, the conteſt.—Negatived:—And laſtly in his motion for peace, May 30th, 1794, the ſame attempt met the ſame fate.

So much for your conduct, in not rendering the war a war of the people, by ſuffering them to underſtand it's purpoſe. But the groſs inconſiſtencies of which you with the miniſter have been guilty, *in order to evade theſe motions*, have not only not raiſed an enthuſiaſm for the war, but rendered your motives ſuſpicious and the war unpopular and hateful. In 1792 you declared peace to be deſirable with France, but that war was to be apprehended from particular acts: yet you refuſed to negotiate with the miniſter of a Republic, the only mode by which peace could be obtained:—and afterwards to make peace when the pretended obſtacles were removed. In the beginning of the year 1793 you declared that you had thought it right " to abſtain from interference in the " internal affairs of France," that the war was " nei-" ther begun nor carried on by this country for the " purpoſe of interfering in the internal polity of " France, or of eſtabliſhing in that country any form " of government whatever, *an object therefore the at-" tainment whereof was not eſſential towards the termina-" tion of the war.*" Yet in the year 1794 you ſay, July 10th, with Mr. Pitt, " that the avowed object
of

"of the war was none of those which had been ascribed to ministers, it was simply the destruction of the system of jacobinism in France;" an object which could not be heightened by new grounds of success, nor relinquished from any temporary failure in it's means of attainment, and was one which he would never depart from, as absolutely necessary to the security and preservation of his country." And who, having declared that this object, which at first was *no object at all*, was an object which was *never to be relinquished*, entered into a negotiation for peace in 1796 and 1797 with the *very jacobins* whom you had so abused.

But it may be asked what purpose equivocation and inconsistency could serve to the minister? It has served the purpose of uniting in a common league, all parties who were from different motives disposed to war. By stating his meaning in lofty but indefinite generalities, Mr. Pitt amused them all, by inducing each to imagine that his particular object was the leading feature of his policy. To the commercial men, it was "indemnity for the past and security for the future." To those who favoured the war, through a mixture of alarm and selfishness, the destruction of the government of France was a "*means* of attaining other ends." Whilst to Mr. Burke it was "the destruction of the system of jacobinism" alone.

Let us now examine whether the conduct of the war

war was calculated to produce, or has obtained, the real or alledged ends of it.

And here give me leave to observe, that this review of history, so far from raising in the minds of Englishmen that sentiment of exultation, and gratitude to Heaven, which we have been commanded to express, by the magnificence of state processions, and the solemnities of religious rites, can only impress it with feelings of humiliation and despair. Or, if it is necessary that we obtrude our cause on the Almighty, it at least should be presented by the spirit and voice of supplication, as a peace-offering of repentance. It is mocking his providence to contradict and gainsay the declarations which it has given of its indignation in those judgments, with which, in every species of calamity and disaster, it has visited this unhappy land. *Nec enim unquam atrocioribus populi Romani cladibus, magisve justis judiciis approbatum est, non esse curæ deis securitatem nostram, esse* ULTIONEM.

First then I will suppose, that Mr. Pitt had nothing in view but the declared objects of the war. Let us take each of these in its date, and compare it with the train of measures undertaken for its accomplishment. I shall begin from the period at which we joined the confederacy against France.

Here then it is to be remembered, that we were entering on an enterprize, in which we were not the first adventurers; we joined others as companions of their way, a part of which we only proposed

to

to travel, but by a common mode of conveyance. A project generally derives its complexion from the characters by whom it is defigned; at leaft men fo often perfonify the opinions they efpoufe, in the eye of the world, as to render it neceffary for us to exercife a little philofophy when we would feparate the actor and the act. Therefore in this inftar :e, it was of fome moment to know, with whofe party and purpofes we had affociated ourfelves; fince "evil communication corrupts good manners;" and (whether owing to this principle, I know not,) but certain it is, that we had our original purpofes and profeffions ftrangely ftolen from us by the way, which we have never fince had t⁺ good fortune to recover.

Now when th. King of Pruffia and the Emperor of Germany declared war againft France, there were, I believe, fome fufpicions entertained as to the difintereftednefs of their views, and the fincerity of their profeffions. They had, it is true, publifhed a manifefto, or rather homily, full of morality, peace and moderation: declaring that they took up arms "to preferve the happinefs and order of the focial world." Like true knights errant, they fallied forth, to redrefs wrongs, heal diffentions, fuccour the diftreffed, refcue civil fociety from the fangs of thofe republican monfters, by whom it was infefted; in fhort to bring down *Aftrea* herfelf once more to the habitations of men. But as nothing can do juftice to this "noble performance" but its own terms, let it fpeak for itfelf.

self. " This manifesto was published to lay open to
" the present generation, as well as to posterity,
" their motives, their designs, and the disinterednefs
" of their personal views; taking up arms for
" the purpose of preserving social order amongst
" all civilized nations, and to secure to each state,
" its religion, happiness, independence, territories,
" and real constitution. On this ground, they
" hoped that all empires and all states ought to
" be unanimous; and becoming the firm guardians
" of the happiness of mankind, that they cannot fail
" to unite their efforts to rescue a numerous nation
" from its own fury, and to preserve Europe from
" the return of barbarism, and the universe from the
" subversion and anarchy with which it was threat-
" ened."

Who would not have armed in such a cause; who would not have subscribed to a manifesto, which breathes the pious zeal of a Godfrey, and the generous policy of a Naffau? Or rather who is here, so lost to sense and virtue, as not to reprobate the stale hypocrisy of a declaration, whose authors had exhibited so recent a specimen of their regard for religious faith, for the independence and true constitution of other countries, when they tore from unhappy Poland her liberty, her constitution, and existence as a nation? " The whole of this noble performance," Mr. Burke says, " should be read at the first con-
" grefs that is held for the general pacification of Eu-
" rope."

F.

"1..pe." And so it should, that it may remind the high contracting parties, that they are *an alliance of sovereign princes*, assembled to restore peace to a bleeding world, and not a *gang of thieves collected to divide a spoil.*

Indeed it is doubtful to this day whether the retreat of the Duke of Brunswick from Champagne was more owing to the abhorrence in which his sovereign masters and their professions were held, or to their own tricking policy and double dealing.

However, England joined the confederacy with at least the profession of *other views and motives* in her mouth, than an interference with the Jacobinical Government. According to her quarrel, therefore, the cause of the emigrants was expressly laid out of the question : it was a question of French and English politics, not an espousal of one party of the French nation against the other—According to our own original statements, it was a war " purely collateral to " the state of Jacobinism, and as much a foreign war " to us and all our home concerns, as the war with " Spain, 1740, about the *Garda Costas*, the Madrid " Convention, or the fable of Captain Jenkins's " ears." When, therefore, the emigrants had experienced the treatment which they had met with, and the mysterious conduct that had been observed by Austria and Prussia in Champagne ; and when they read your reasons for war in your diplomatic correspondence, and senatorial debates ; could it be expected ed that they would co-operate heartily with you, or attempt a serious movement in France under such auspices? But to crown the whole, the Prince of Saxe Cobourg issued a proclamation upon Dumourier's desertion, inviting the French nation to rally round the constitution of 1789; and when he found that Dumourier had not as many sympathisers in treason as he expected, he revoked this declaration, and seized on Condé and Valenciennes, *in the name and right of his Majesty the Emperor.*

What could you expect from such weak and perfidious conduct? Such was the disgust and dread excited against you in the French nation, that under the most cruel tyranny which the world ever saw, they flew to arms, and buried in their resolution not to be conquered, all memory of having been oppressed!

So that at the close of the campaign of 1793, you were nearly in point of local situation, where the Duke of Brunswick was previous to his retreat from France. But with this difference; that then the emigrants were with you, the royalists in France were with you; your resources were entire; your armies compleat—whilst France was a divided people, without armies and without money to oppose you;— and now when you had spent millions, and sacrificed thousands of lives, the French had united her people, armed and disciplined the population of the country, and succeeded, by the terrible energy of a revolutionary

ary Government, in bringing into action the collective capital of the nation.

To this success *you* had principally contributed—for if you had been sincere in your alledged grounds of complaint and war, it is evident that you would have sought for peace when these objects were attained: but so far from this, when Holland was free from danger, the decree of the 19th of November repealed, and the French power crippled by the success of the allies, when consequently your pretended objects of war were obtained, instead of seeking peace, you take a fresh ground of hostility, and now contend for " *indemnity for the past and security for the future.*"

Thus then a suspicion, fatal to *their* views, was cast on *the coalesced powers*, from the nature of *your objects* in the war, inasmuch as they were distinct from, nay according to your language, opposed to, a restoration of the antient Government of France. And from your co-operation with a party who *professed to interfere in her internal affairs*, you in your turn became justly an object of suspicion. Thus whilst your contrary principles of action weakened the general effect of the arms of the allies; the French Government was enabled to say of *you* in particular, to her own people: ' see what is the pretended sincerity of the English Go-
' vernment, she disclaims interference in our domestic
' affairs, yet she joins a party whose avowed object it is
to

'to interfere; she goes to war on one ground, and
'no sooner is that removed, and an opportunity of-
'fered her of proving the sincerity of her declarations,
'than she takes another ground; judge you then
'whether it is to your own or the English Government
'that you owe the evils of war; the one has always
'sought peace on one plain and uniform principle,
'the other has enlarged her pretensions, and changed
'her ground with every turn of good fortune.'

Such had been the success and tendency of your conduct down to the close of the year 1793, that the revolutionary sentiment was strengthened in the hearts of Frenchmen, and views of future aggrandizement rendered more distinct and sanguine in the minds of their rulers.

At length you avowed, that " the destruction of the Jacobin system was the object of the war," and the *sine qua non* of pacification. But your general treatment of the Royalist party, your declaration that their cause was only an instrument to obtain other ends, and your treachery at Toulon, had alienated them from your interest. You had told them before, that an interference in their internal affairs was only a *means to answer other purposes*. What purposes? why to obtain "indemnity for the past and security for the future." What indemnity could you expect? Not money, for that you denied that she possessed, in all your reasonings on the finances of France; but

she

she had colonial possessions, and they had from the beginning dazzled the eye of your ambition. What security? The annihilation of French power and independence, when she was portioned out, and garrisoned by your allies; that was your security: yes, you fought *in her plunder for your indemnity, and for your security in her ruin!* In the sincerity of my heart I rejoice, when I look back on the whole of this detestable plot, engendered in *that* mind, that is bloated with arrogant projects, that the over-ruling providence has made the violation of its laws, and the profanation of its name, its own peculiar avengement—that it has withered the arm of human strength, and confounded those impious politics, whose triumph must have been b'  on the overthrow of man's independenc., on the __. of his liberty and reason.

And how did you accredit the declaration of Downing Street? You not only did not give the Emigrants, the place, which the first party to your new cause was entitled to, but you did not in misfortune incurred on your behalf, shew them a decent consideration. Instead of protecting that unhappy body of men, on your retreat in 1794, you every where left them to defend places which you knew could not be maintained; and which on their surrender must expose these betrayed wretches to certain ·' struction. It will be reserved to the pen of indignant history, when the motives of men, and the

events

events of measures shall be more clearly developed, to do justice to the foul proceedings of the Allies. —To hold up to deserved detestation the whole conspiracy of those iniquitous politicians, by whom, those brave but unfortunate gentlemen, who in exile had nothing left them but their swords and their principles, were coldly and cruelly sacrificed to selfish ends, to false pretences, and to wicked, because chimerical experiments. But why should we be so romantic as to complain that the loss of honour, and the effusion of human blood, do not disturb the complacent calculations of cabinets and statesmen!

What a contemptible figure therefore did our councils now make in the eyes of Europe! Exactly as the train of events gradually rendered it more and more impracticable to accomplish the overthrow of the French government, in that proportion you bound yourselves incontinently to pursue it. In the beginning of 1793 it was at least a feasible project. Then you renounced it altogether. In the course of the campaign it became more difficult; you were then suspected of having it in view. It soon grew to be a forlorn hope; then you declared it to be a desirable *means* of accomplishing your original end. And at length when it was hopeless; you avowed, that you would not lay down your arms until it was accomplished. Yet strange to tell, so much is inconsistency your

fate,

fate, that you have been compelled to withdraw your haughty pledge, to unsay your arrogant declaration, and to sue for peace to the agents and system of jacobinism!* to have your overtures and your ambassador treated with contempt and insult; and to hear the very language from the mouth of your enemy that so lately was in your own. For the *delenda Carthago* once so familiar to English tongues, is now translated into the French language.

For now the French in their turn declare, that they will not make peace with your government. The war has therefore become (dreadful to say) literally a war of extermination. It becomes you then to examine into the state of your remaining power, and compare it with the resources and condition of the enemy. It would be as useless as criminal to palliate and conceal misfortune. We must confess with Mr. Burke, that the Jacobins " have seen the thing right " from the beginning." For whilst you have failed in almost every instance, they have succeeded even in those romantic projects of aggrandizement, which were at first attributed to them by very few indeed. You went to war with them to defend an ally; he has been conquered, and become an ally of France:— to protect the rights of neutral nations; and there is

---

* Out of the eight Directors with whom you have negotiated, four voted for the death of the King, viz. Barras, Carnot, Reveillere, Lépaux, Merlin of Douay.

scarce

scarce a power in Europe that has not been compelled to declare war against you;—to defend religion, and half Europe is secularized;—to secure property, and Italy, Holland, Belgium, Germany, Spain, have been laid under contribution;—to prevent their plans of aggrandizement, and they have changed places with you in the scale of alliances; whilst they have subjected the Netherlands, Holland, Italy, Spain, and part of Germany to their power. To check the spread of revolutionary sentiment, and the evil which before the war was confined to correspondences between the clubs of London and Paris, is now established by a *balance of republican interest*, connected with a *balance of power*, that outweighs the rest of monarchical and aristocratical Europe.

To compensate these losses, you have at an enormous expence of blood and treasure obtained the minister's favourite foreign object, an accession of colonial territory, and an advantage in the balance of trade. But let any man, that reflects on the principle of European colonization, cast his eye on the price which the maintenance of the West Indies alone has cost this country, in the course of the present century; let him recollect, that our conquests there and elsewhere, are still in the contemplation, and subject to the contingencies of a future negotiation for peace; let him look too at the line of coast, and the immense foundation for a future maritime power, which France possesses *absolutely*; and then determine on the value

of

of these considerations. In addition, however, to this object, we have added to our former naval renown, by the most splendid victories. Certainly we have; and every Englishman ought to contemplate with pride, the naval triumphs of his country. But still these successes, for which his Majesty and all the state have been pleased to exhibit a grand spectacle to the city of London, remind me, under the present circumstances of the country, of the old story of the giant and the dwarf. They both gained the victory, it is true, but the giant only enjoyed it: for the poor dwarf had suffered so much in the contest, that when it was over, he died. So I fear it will prove with the people of this country: they gain a great deal of honour, but in the mean time they are ruined and starved.

As this is a war of the governments, it is desirable to oppose France with an opposite principle and party. But where can you look for them now? Where are the insurgents of Toulon, of Marseilles, of Lyons? Where the Christian army of La Vendée, its leaders and chiefs? Where is that Charette, whom a confidence in you betrayed to an ignominious end, who in the bitterness of his soul, poured out curses on your government, with his dying breath? Where is the gallant, the ill fated, Sombrieul? But that is a tale that should dye the British cheek with eternal shame: whilst in the royalist party, it has converted confidence into distrust, and gratitude into

hatred

hatred and revenge; deceived so often, they will trust their betrayers no more.

To foreign aids you can look no longer; your allies are every where become your secret or open enemies. Such has been the nature and the result of the minister's miserable and wicked policy, *that he has done for France exactly that, which you went to war with her for having designed and imagined.* There never was so great a Jacobin, or at least so great a friend to the Jacobins, in conduct, as Mr. Pitt. He has been an instrument in their hands, to effect their purposes, whilst by his intentions and motives, he has raised in them an implacable spirit of hatred and revenge against himself and the country. Yet this is the man who calls as loudly and arrogantly for confidence, who challenges enquiry as boldly into his conduct, and appeals to events, now t! they have proved one tissue of disasters and disgraces, with as much unblushing impudence, as he did, when he swayed the destinies of Europe, and made the French republic tremble for her existence. There is not one object of the war gained by him; yet there never was such a power of instrument and means committed to the hands of a European governor!—There is r instance of failure both in design, and in execution, of which he has not been convicted; there is no calamity which he has not inflicted on his country; and yet he obstinately holds the reins of office, with the same lofty tone of presumption, and the same hardi-

hood

hood of resolve, as ever ; and still at the annual opening of his *Pandora's* box, entertains the *representatives of the people* with a long and eloquent romance on the prosperous state of the country.

" *Populus me sibilat, sed mihi plaudo,*" is indeed his motto and maxim.

But to you, who pledged your lives and fortunes, for the maintenance of this war, I beg leave to address a few considerations, that I think if rightly understood, and if attended to in time, will awaken you to the state of danger, into which this magician of the state has lulled you by his plausible, but deceitful eloquence. Gentlemen, there is all the need in the world, for you now to come forward with the stake of your *lives and fortunes*. *You had better risk the whole than lose it.* And if you continue to sleep on as now you do, a time will come, when you will be aroused by a storm, that will sweep away your " lives and your fortunes."

I have hitherto adverted to the folly or the hypocrisy of which you have been guilty in your motives for entering into the war ; to the actual results of it's management, as it affects your external interest ; and to the proof which this history affords, of the wickedness, the incapacity, and ruinous perseverance of the Minister.

But important as these considerations doubtless would have been at another time, they are reduced to " parochial insignificance" compared with the

more

more pressing and alarming dangers of the day. It has been said that the signs of the times are visible to common eyes, when Empires totter and nations verge to decay. Is not the writing on the wall against us? Have we not reason for alarm, not only on account of the ambition of an enemy, but the full maturity of those seeds of destruction, which, with parricidal hands, the sons of England have sown in the heart of their country?

First we are to resist France—She declares she will not make peace with your government, in 1797—You declared that you would not lay down your arms until you had destroyed her's in 1793. So much for the *lex talionis*. Each government is quite mad and wicked enough. On what ground did you found your hopes of success; on what ground do they found theirs? You hoped it from the internal disturbances and dissensions by which she was distracted, in consequence of the oppressions and miseries she suffered from her government; and from the ruin of her finances, which you conceived to be the " nerves and sinews of war."—She *precisely hopes the same effects from the same causes*. Your expectations have been disappointed. Is there such an analogy between the case of France in 1793, and of England in 1797, as to give us good ground to hope, that France will meet the same fate?

Why did your hopes fail?—From two causes.

1st. A miscalculation of her means and resources;

and,

and, 2dly. An ignorance of the state of the public opinion.

1st. You miscalculated her means and resources. It was not only in this country but throughout Europe the fashion, both before and after the war, to prophesy the destruction of the French finances, and to ridicule as absurd and impolitic their scheme of paper currency. On the contrary, however, amongst the discoveries which time will make, and the prejudices that experience will remove, one of the first in political affairs, will be perhaps this error on the nature and policy of the *assignats* of France. So far from it's having been a poor expedient and inefficient contrivance, that could serve the purpose of the government for a little time only: it appears to me to have been one of the profoundest strokes of policy, as well as one of the most succesful engines, to obtain and secure power, that has been invented by man. Its authors seem purposely to have given to it so much *appearance of analogy in it's principle, to the principle of the funding system, or of general paper credit*, as to deceive the rest of Europe into an opinion that it's success, nature, and effects might be appreciated on the same grounds, and by the same criterion, viz. it's relation to the value of money, or other representative signs of property. And that, therefore, in proportion as it was depreciated or rose in value, according to that test, it was nearer or further from extinction. Now why was this reasoning false? Because it went on the suppofition, that only a certain quantity of affignats were iffued; and then it muft follow, that if fifty thoufand at a certain rate of value, are neceffary as a circulating medium, when thefe by depreciation become worth no more than 25,000, they are by the proportion of one half unequal to the purpofes of circulation. But what was the fact? The French did not limit their iffues, by any other rule than the rate of the affignat; therefore, if by depreciation to day, fifty affignats are only worth as much as one was yefterday, and to-morrow a thoufand fhall be only worth fifty; they had nothing to do but to *make up in quantity what they loft in value*, and multiply them fifty, a thoufand, or an hundred thoufand times if neceffary: therefore, whilft the affignat was *worth any thing*, it was the fame to them, as long as they had paper and ink, whether it was worth a *livre* or a *louis d'or*. At length the affignats were worth nothing: what then? Did the government fall? No fuch thing: it never was fo ftrong and flourifhing as at the prefent moment. But ftill the affignats would not ferve to pay the armies, or purchafe the foreign commodities, of which, from the ftate of their country, the French ftood in need. What refource had they in this cafe? *Bullion*. It is well known, that at the time when you both in and out of Parliament, were expecting to hear by every mail, of the ruin of her finances—that the French treafury was overflowing with *fpecie*. According to M. Calonne's account,

(a man

(a man who from his fortunes and opinions is not likely to exaggerate the ſtrength of the Republic) ſhe had, either ſecreted, in circulation, or in the hands of the government 120,000,000l. ſterling of ſpecie. "Thus" ſays he, " Becauſe the dreadful extortions, and a
" monſtrous profuſion of paper money made the
" *ſpecie* diſappear, we conclude that there is none re-
" maining in the kingdom ; though it is evident that
" of *one hundred and twenty millions ſterling* in gold and
" ſilver *ſpecie*, that exiſted before the revolution, ſup-
" poſing that there were forty millions exported either
" by the emigrants or for the purpoſe of purchaſing
" foreign commodities, or for the purpoſe of bribery ;
" and even without reckoning what has been obtain-
" ed by the forced contributions of the conquered
" countries—Yet even on this ſuppoſition, there muſt
" remain in France about *eighty millions ſterling in*
" *ſpecie*. We do not include in this calculation all
" the plate and precious ornaments poſſeſſed by ſo
" many individuals, and by fifty-two thouſand
" churches or convents, which cannot be valued with
" preciſion, but which muſt have been very con-
" ſiderable. Whatever has been coined ſince the
" revolution muſt likewiſe be added to it; and
" every thing conſidered, it cannot be queſtioned,
" that by reducing to eighty millions ſterling, all the
" gold and ſilver of every denomination, coined or
" not, now exiſting in France, we are rather below
" than above the real ſum. Such a ſum would certainly

" tainly be sufficient for France, since in England it is
" reckoned that thirty-five millions only are in cir-
" culation."

What immense power then must have resulted from this scheme to the rulers of the day, since by supplying, and forcing on the country, a new circulating medium, they were enabled to reserve whatever part of this capital remained, and a large part it must have been, for the external exigencies of the State. By this she has maintained her armies— by this she has obtained the necessary commodities of foreign countries; and by this, on the event of a peace, she may be enabled to re-establish the system of her internal industry to an extent, and on principles of which we are little aware.

You have then clearly been erroneous in *your* calculations on her finances—Are *her* ideas of the state of yours equally unfounded.

What is their state? The national Debt of England amounts nearly to the enormous sum of 400,000,000; to pay the interest of which 15,000,000, must be yearly deducted from the productive industry of the country.—I shall not enter into the question of the advantage or disadvantage of a national debt, although I conceive it has been proved to demonstration by Dr. Smith, that it is the cause of the high price of provisions according to the vulgar notion, or to speak more correctly, of the depreciation of the value of *specie*: and consequently that it has in that proportion diminished the value of your capital, or in

fact abforbed fo much of it. But be that as it may, you are now reduced to fuch a ftate as to your funding fyftem, that you *dare* not draw on it for your fupplies any longer; fince ftocks which were at 96 in 1789, are now at 49 and a fraction; you are therefore compelled to exact 7,000,000 more within the year, *if you can raife it*, by the new mode of tripling the affeffed taxes. Which added to the intereft of the public debt amounts to the fum of 22,000,000.\*
—The whole fuppofed capital in *fpecie* in this country amounts to 35,000,000. So that only 13,000,000 are not drawn into the channels of taxation. It will here perhaps be faid, but France according to your own arguments, has been able to furvive a greater paper currency, and a more enormous public expenditure. And upon this *nominal* comparifon have all the falfe calculations of minifters on the ftate of the finances of the two countries been built. You confounded the *nominal* with the *relative* value of the affignat. " And thence " inferred, that the expences of France in one month " are greater than thofe of England for one year; " and that the expences of the French for one year " furpafs the whole national debt of England." So fay my Lords Mornington and Auckland; what fays truth? Why certainly that as from the former ftatement of the depreciation of the affignats,

\* The intereft of the Loan of 12,000,000, is not here included. That muft be alfo added to make the account of our finances compleat.

the

"the 30,000 millions or 1,200 millions sterling,
"expended by France, since the beginning of the
"revolution, represent now, but 150,000,000 of
"*specie*, or six millions sterling, it follows that the
"four campaigns, &c. have not cost France the fourth
"part of what England expends in one year of the
"war?"—There is therefore no analogy, (or if
any it is, according to the reasoners against the assignats, against us) between the state of our finances
now, and those of France at any period of her paper
circulation. There is none moreover, from their
opposite natures, for their paper currency proceeded
on the principle of supplying the deficiency of value
by quantity, ours proceeds on the principle of supplying the deficiency of quantity, by the excellence
of public credit. The moment therefore this bulwark
is broken in on, the system of the English funds will
tumble to the ground: and it is no exaggeration to
say, great *for many reasons* will be the fall thereof.

Our hopes of a counter-revolution also failed
because you were ignorant of the state of the public
opinion, or at least did not know the effects of revolutionary sentiment when organized and in a state
of practice. First you reasoned, as if it was natural
for a people to resist or to revolt from the oppressions
of a new, as readily as of an old government. Now
mankind are naturally prone to novelty and change:
the French had then undergone the most cruel
oppression from the old *regime*, and therefore
the oppression of the new had not the effect on

their minds and habits, that it would have had on a people familiarized to a state of liberty and social comfort. They, in the next place, had experienced the stability of the old despotism; and from the nature of the new, as being a state of anarchy, they might reasonably hope that it would not long continue. Besides, they saw that the existence of the new order of things was identified with their national independence. For your conduct, and that of your allies, had taught them what to expect on the event of a counter-revolution. Your hopes again were disappointed, because you judged of the means of a revolutionary, by the criterions and tests of regular governments. In the regular governments of Europe, *the social effort has been a collection of individual efforts, bottomed on individual or selfish motives: in France, all individuality has been lost sight of, in the singleness and generality of the public movement.* " When
" I contemplate, says Mr. Burke, the scheme on
" which France is formed, and when I compare
" it with these systems with which it is, and ever must
" be in conflict, those things which seem as defects
" in her polity, are the very things which make me
" tremble. The states of the Christian world have
" grown up to their present magnitude in a great space
" of time, and by a great variety of accidents. They
" have been improved to what we see them, with
" greater or less degrees of felicity and skill. Not
" one of them has been formed upon a regular plan,
" or

" or with any unity of defign. As their conftitutions
" are not fyftematical, they have not been directed
" to any *peculiar* end, eminently diftinguifhed, and
" fuperfeding every other. The objects which they
" embrace, are of the greateft poffible variety, and
" have become in a manner infinite. In all thefe old
" countries, the *ftate has been made to the people, and
" not the people conformed to the ftate.* Every ftate has
" purfued, not only every fort of focial advantage,
" but it has cultivated the welfare of every indivi-
" dual. This comprehenfive fcheme, virtually pro-
" duced a degree of perfonal liberty in forms the
" moft adverfe to it. That liberty was found in mo-
" narchies the moft abfolute, in a degree unknown to
" the antient commonwealths. From hence the power
" of all our modern ftates meet, in their movements,
" with fome obftruction. It is therefore no wonder,
" *that when thefe ftates are to be confidered as machines
" to operate for fome one great end, that this diffipated and
" balanced force is not eafily concentered, or made to bear
" with the whole nation, upon one point, &c.*"

" But in France the will, the wifh, the want, the
" liberty, the toil, the blood of individuals is nothing.
" Individuality is left out of their fcheme of govern-
" ment. The ftate is all in all. Every thing is re-
" ferred to the production of force; afterwards every
" thing is trufted to the ufe of it. It is military in its
" principle, in its maxims, in its fpirit, and in all its
" movements." Such then as has been ably defcribed

by

by Mr. Burke, is the genius of a revolutionary government.

The fame means of refiftance you clearly have not, becaufe you want the leading principle of this energy. "For "fays Mr. Burke," the Britifh Senate is with out "queftion, that which purfues the greateft variety of "ends, and is the leaft difpofed to facrifice any one "of them to another or to the whole. It aims at "taking in the entire circle of human defires, and "fecuring for them their fair enjoyment. Our legif- "lature has been ever clofely connected it its moft "efficient part with *individual* feeling, and *individual* "intereft, &c. On this principle, therefore, England "would be the weakeft power of the whole fyftem."

But you have alfo made a falfe eftimate of the powers which this principle of unity and indivifibility could call into action; and they are fuch as a State founded on the fame relations as thofe of the Englifh State, cannot command and employ. We never confidered the power of a State, which was able and daring enough to lay hold on the phyfical refources of the country, who has feized on nature itfelf.— "She had her territorial productions for her own fub- "fiftence, her men to recruit her armies, her wool "to furnifh them with cloathing, her iron to fupply "her youth with arms, her horfes to remount her "cavalry, and her fanaticifm to give a new elaftic "fpring to her courage."*—And thefe fhe accord-

* Calonne's Political State of Europe.

ingly seized on, on the *totality* of them. But your efforts, from the controul of your political and social habitudes, must be the result of partial dispositions and individual contributions; therefore, in respect to *means*, there is no analogy between you and revolutionary France. You have, if you please, *money* and *art*—they had *arms* and *men*.

I have before said that you failed from a misconception of the state and motives of her public sentiment; but, I did not then shew why there was not an analogy sufficiently strong between the cases of the two countries in this respect, for it to prove conclusively, that she would *therefore* be equally disappointed. I did not then discuss this part of my subject, because as it is the most material of our many important domestic considerations, I wished to reserve it to the conclusion of my address to you, that it may be impressed on your minds as strongly, as the slender talents of the writer will enable him to enforce it. For it is indeed the most serious subject of concern to all men who love the country and covet peace, but to you, it is no less an object than your *social existence*.

In turning my eyes therefore to the internal interests of the country, a view of them may be taken under two points, the *government* and the *governed.* For this i every country must be the sum of it's social relations. When, therefore, I see my country placed in the alarming situation in which it now stands, I could have wished that the foundation and

principle

principle of those relations had been found and entire. That the constitution of which we boast so much, and in many respects so justly, had been in all its parts, deserving the proud and enviable distinction which it has acquired, viz. the envy and admiration of the world. That in this age of theories and experiments in civil government, the model of English liberty, if it was less daring and brilliant than others, might yet obtain the applause and preference of the judgment, from the more sedate but valuable qualities of rational liberty and substantial usefulness. That the writings of Montesquieu and De Lolme would be no longer read as the ingenious disquisitions of learned men, but that the experiments of an enlightened age would add the *fiat* of experience to the sanctions of philosophy and speculation. I did hope, that if the government rested on it's legitimate foundation, if it's administration was directed to the happiness of the people, the people on their part would by a character and conduct worthy the genius of a free nation, have displayed the eager and virtuous enthusiasm which they ought to feel for such a blessing, and would have treated with indignation and contempt, the menace of an enemy to overthrow it by foreign force, and with just and condign punishment, the attempts of domestic traitors, whether in or out of office, to corrupt it's principles and change it's nature. But it seems in this country, that to express a virtuous regard for the public weal, a love of liberty, and a

sincere

sincere conviction that public and private duties can form but one code of morals, is a romantic and puerile enthusiasm. It is suited indeed to the imagination of a school boy, warm from the perusal of antient story, filled with examples of antient patriotism, and with maxims and images of antient freedom: but it argues a want of *knowledge of the world*, of men and manners, of observation and experience, to indulge in these scholastic reveries, to carry them forward with you into real life, or to dream that their lofty illus— are consistent with the capacities and condition of man. If it is so, I must be content to abide the censure of the world. For never can I so far forget those sacred lessons of virtue which my early youth imbibed from the oracles of the antient world, those recitals of great exploit and heroic suffering, in defence of freedom; and the whole system of thought and action, which was founded on the principle of a delightful and expanded benevolence, as to deride and deny their value. To those stores of memory I turn my mind, when it is sick with the contemplation of human misery and crime: not that it may forget itself or human nature; but that it may be stimulated to virtuous exertion, and be consoled for the degradation of man, as he is, by contemplating the picture of what he has been, and the hope of what he may be.

But these ideas are not romantic; the providence which governs the affairs of men, has wisely and benevolently decreed, that its laws should be the paths of happiness. It has erected, even here, an

I awful

awful principle of moral retribution, that acts as unerringly on the affairs of states, as on the actions of private men. And never has it or will it suffer a violation of the principles of justice and virtue, to be a means of permanent prosperity to either one or the other. True greatness therefore, and indeed lasting safety, must be looked for, from an adherence to the principles of justice. Does the state of these kingdoms, of its government and people, warrant us in hoping that we have a right to expect either greatness or safety? Has the former acted the part of so faithful a guardian of the welfare of the latter, that in danger and distress it should conceive itself entitled to a return of support and protection? Has it, as it ought to have been, proved the nurse and not the destroyer of public virtue? For it is an eternal truth, that the government of every country is the cause of the moral and political habitudes of the people. The invariable testimony of history proves that those countries which have been blessed with pure and just systems of political institution, have been distinguished by a corresponding spirit and character in the people. For in free governments, the public mind is early imbued with the invigorating motive of public spirit, and disciplined in the school of generous and elevated principle; it is taught to cherish as an instinct an interest in the public welfare; to consider as the highest destination of human effort, situations of public trust and power; to look

with

with reverence to the virtuous examples of the dead, and with emulation to those of the living. Thus then patriotism becomes the ruling passion of such a nation; because an exercise of its duties is the only path to distinction, or happiness; for in a society which is governed by such a mode of public opinion, the censorial power that is generated by it, makes selfishness and vice too painful punishments for them to have many votaries: and government therefore if it is good, will necessarily produce a general observance of the laws of morality. "As well might we "fancy that of itself the sea will swell, and that "without the winds, the billows will insult the "adverse shore, as that the gross of the people will be "moved and elevated and continue by a steady and "permanent direction to bear on one point, without "the influence of superior authority of superior "mind."

I am sure then, that if this doctrine be just, if the temper and habits of a people are derived from their government, the aspect of English society is not very favourable to the credit of English government. You who have so long complained of the corruption of the people, who have so long reiterated it as an argument against reforms that have been proposed by wiser and better men than yourselves, take shame for having been the authors of that corruption. As well might the assassin deride the efforts which were made to heal the wounds that he had inflicted, because they were desperate, as you persecute and revile those who would reform the government, because the people are corrupt.

It is indeed, a melancholy truth, that the people are corrupt, that the people are indifferent to what concerns their nearest interest; that the moral sense is as dead in them, as the springs of social action are relaxed and debilitated. But you, who once valued yourselves on this acquiescence, who construed it into the popularity of your measures; who praised the good sense, and sober character of Englishmen, who ridiculed and persecuted those who (though perhaps mistaken) complained of and endeavoured to stimulate their torpor, do you now acknowledge the justice of these complaints. The people are longer called on by the London Corresponding Society to assert their liberties: they are no longer tempted to acts of sedition by inflammatory hand-bills; but they are called on by the voice of their rulers, of the government, of the titled and propertied orders of the community. And still the people are " like the deaf adder, that " hears not the voice of the charmer, charm he ne- " ver so wisely." This is undoubtedly to be deplored; but is not to be wondered at: look at the history of the administration of this government for the last century; look to its progress, more particularly for the last six years, and you will be no longer at a loss for the solution of this ænigma.

How has the administration of the government affected

fected public happiness, for that is its end and criterion, since the revolution of 1688? Public happiness, may not perhaps, be improperly said to consist of two things: Liberty and Security. The great means by which the liberty of this country seems to me to have been affected, has been from the consequences that have resulted from the enormous influence of your public debt. It has, I conceive, produced two effects: its interest, which is the revenue of the country, from its mode of collection and disposition, has enabled the minister of the day to acquire such an ascendancy over the legislature, as to subject the constitution to his controul: and, in this respect, each succeeding minister has been more successful than his predecessor, from the increase of his means. And in the second place, the capital of the debt has involved such an immense mass of public interest in its preservation or destruction, that inasmuch as those events depend on the stability of the government, and that government, from the preceding argument is in a state of monopoly, the interests of an immense class of citizens are nearly identified with those of the minister of the day. This has induced, in my opinion, the whole of that long and immense detail of incroachments on popular right and liberty, with which the present century, and particularly our own times, have abounded. The consequence of a loss of liberty is naturally attended with an indifference to it; and a preponderance of those selfish motives, by which

which at firſt that liberty had been overthrown. Or rather, it would be more correct to ſay, that the ſubſtitution of a ſyſtem of ſelfiſh motives, in the room of ſocial, deſtroys that *ſpirit of liberty*, which Lord Bolingbroke has juſtly ſaid, is not only that, without which forms of government or law are a dead letter; but that, which, without forms of government or law, at ſome time or other, will enable the people to aſſert their rights. But it may be obſerved, alſo, that although inſtitutions and forms of freedom are produced by its ſpirit, yet that when created, they react on the ſpirit of liberty, by infuſing into it from time to time, the vigour and energy that are eſſential to its exiſtence. Hence Machiavel obſerves, that thoſe governments are beſt, which are drawn back the ofteneſt to their original principles. For the form is the ſign and character of the principle; and in government, as well as religion, externals are of ſovereign uſe. But in this country, it has been as vain for a long time paſt to look for the form of liberty as its ſpirit: there is ſcarce a ſingle barrier which our anceſtors planted againſt the encroachments of the crown, that has not been removed; and although ſome ceremonies of the old worſhip of freedom are preſerved, its ſpirit and devotion are, alas! extinct in the people.

There is another conſequence from the predominance of ſelfiſh intereſts, which is, that the ſpirit of liberty, which has been really dead, has been ſupplied by a baſtard principle, the ſpirit of faction. " Octavius " has a party in the ſenate, and ſo has Anthony, but
" the

"but the commonwealth has none." That feeling or concern for political affairs, which should have been a general interest, has become a personal attachment. And the consequence has been, that as all the leaders of parties have had equally the language of liberty in their mouths when out of office, and betrayed its interests when in; the people from finding all professions equally false, and all public men equally perfidious, have at last grown into a belief, that all politics are equally dishonest, and every patriot equally insincere.

But these evils, although destructive of public happiness, have been slow in their growth, and insensible in their approaches. There is another, and well I am convinced, that it is the most alarming evil if rightly considered which can light on a country circumstanced as this is, that appears likely to result from the posture of your finances, and the burthens which are about to be laid on the people.

I cannot say that this evil is of sudden growth, because it certainly has been in a less degree apparent for a long time past; although you were either unwilling or unable to trace its real cause or to remove it. It is the destruction of those *Republican manners* which our social relations had produced and perpetuated: the strength, the *stamina*, the pillar, the fountain head of old English hardihood of character. It is this glorious principle that has resisted the influence of those causes, which have in other countries

wrought

wrought the fall of Empires—that has enabled you so often to repair your losses; and to arise with unsubdued energy, from each succeffive difafter. It is this which has preferved amidft your people in the bofom of corruption, and even " luxurious effeminacy" their virtue; from that happy temper, which combined the excellencies of the more civilized and the ruder ftates of fociety; which united the "elegant humanities" of refinement, with the independent virtues of fimplicity; which prevented the people on one hand from finking into ferocity and groffnefs; and on the other the higher orders of the ftate from being corrupted by the infuence of that corporation fpirit, which their nominal diftinction from the people might otherwife have infpired. For it was the rare and happy fortune of this nation, to prefent on the fame day, the fpectacle of a government compofed of the moft ariftocratical relations, and a fociety governed by the fpirit of the moft abfolute equality. The Peer and the Prince were the Peer and the Prince only, when cloathed in their robes of ftate, and invefted with the functions of their political capacities; but, when they ceafed to legiflate, to reprefent the authorities of the nation, they laid afide their dignities and diftinctions, at the threfhold of the fenate, and returned to the great mafs of the people, and to the enjoyment of focial comforts, and the exercife of focial duties, as mere private men. Hence although they at particular feafons, acted the part of a clafs,

and

and caſt of ſeparate and inſulated intereſts, and affected the feelings and the language of ſuch a character; yet it was mimitic and not real: the habits of their lives, their affections, their paſſions, their connexions, all that ſweetens and adorns exiſtence, centered in the people. On the other hand, the gradations of ſociety from the higheſt to the loweſt, were ſo ſmooth and gentle, that the approach of the private citizen to the noble, was eaſy and familiar. The *gentleman* of ſmall but independant fortune, the merchant or the opulent tradeſman, even the Engliſh yeoman, ſaw aſſembled at their board, all ranks of ſociety; and the charm of ſocial intercourſe effectually wore away all remembrance of his ſuperiority from the mind of the Peer, and all ſenſe of inferior condition from the mind of the peaſant. Hence oppreſſion was prevented on one part, and malignant envy and hatred on the other. And it is this principle, the characteriſtic of Engliſh life, that has held together the frame of your government, that has made the governed attached to its form, and patient of it's reſtraint, and the governors attentive to the feelings, the declared opinions and known intereſts of the people.

*Facies non omnibus una,*
*Nec diverſa, tamen qualis decet eſſe ſororum.*

It is with the ſincereſt grief of heart that I have long ſeen the vital principle of this ſyſtem faſt wearing away; and it is with dread, that in the new mode of finance

finance, I contemplate the power, that " at one fell fweep," will efface all that remains of the charities and habitudes of Englifh fociety.

For by impofing fuch burthens on the people, you take from them the power of maintaining their former connexion and intercourfe with the higher orders. You take away that fyftem of habits that has been the nurfe of reciprocal attachment and fympathy. And man is the creature of habits. Other modes of life will induce other opinions. When once a man is reduced to plebeian circumftance, he imbibes plebeian malignity; when he is no longer able to contemplate his fuperior in the amiable light of a private friend and a kind neighbour; when he no longer meets him in the midft of domeftic endearments, and focial charities, exercifing the duties of a father, a hufband, the mafter of a family, or an indulgent landlord; he no longer remembers any thing but his invidious fuperiority, he thinks only of him as a being cloathed with power and fplendour, invefted with the authorities of the ftate, and bleffed with enjoyments, of which he is, as he conceives, unjuftly deprived. Dreadful therefore is the influence of fevere taxation on a free people, becaufe it undermines thofe fecurities on which the energy of that freedom muft of neceffity depend: for what will it avail us, that Weftminfter Hall ftands where it did, that the letter of the conftitution, and the ftatute book remain as they have been in ages paft, if thofe manners, that fpirit, and
that

that national character are no more, which were the parents, and which must be the supports of their existence. Laws and institutions are only instrumental: it is the wisdom, the reason, and the will of the nation from whence they sprung, that are the first causes and the active principles of their utility.

*Quid valeant leges sine moribus*

is as true in Great Britain as it was at Rome.

It remains to me, to examine in what manner the security of the people has been respected by the government; or in other words, in what manner their lives and property have been protected by it! I know that to express a general abhorrence of the war system, to enlarge on its mischiefs and crime, to expose the depraved inconsistency of institutions, which punish with death and infamy the wretch who is driven to the commission of a single murder, by want or any other dire necessity, and which at the same time give the word to slaughter thousands of the human race, and lay waste the fairest scenes of God's creation, for the cold-blooded purposes of speculative policy, is to be guilty of an absurd and irrational fanaticism. Mankind are unfortunately so familiarized to the tale and spectacle of slaughter, that their most virtuous sensibilities are corrupted by those passions of glory, which the names of their destroyers awaken, and the recital of their exploits inflame.

Yet, surely, when we read the apologies for systematic massacre, with which our libraries, our senate, and even our churches, abound, to which the energies of reason, the charms of eloquence, and even the divine authority of the gospel have been made subservient, we must either be convulsed with shame and grief, if what they say is true, or if it be false, tremble with virtuous indignation at the " self-abuse," the mischievous falsehood, and blasphemous hypocrisy of which man is guilty. Is destruction the law of our nature, the necessity of our condition, the original sin of providence itself? Is that only criminal which is committed in paltry detail, when it is glorious in gross and on system? Does the same voice that brought the glad tidings of peace and salvation to man, whose great commandment was universal love, whose gospel came with healing on its wings, and whose author is himself the prince of peace, the brightest, the purest, example of patient and long suffering benevolence; is that voice to blow the trumpet of war, and sound the charge of hatred and bloodshed to the frantic nations? When such doctrines are held in the face, and to the insult of the feelings and the reason of an enlightened age, when that age acts on them, surely these are the tricks which the fools of nature play before high heaven, and which may well make angels weep to contemplate them. But, be that as it may, in common prudence, how can we boast of the security which

we

we have enjoyed, when out of a century our lives and property have been fubject to the diforders and dangers of forty-feven years of warfare? When in confequence of the wars in which we have been engaged and that in which we are engaged, 26,000,000 are to be deducted yearly from the produce of the induftry of the people.

Such is the cafe of the governed; as to their liberty, their morals, their public fpirit, and their general happinefs: what is the ftate of the government?

Never furely was there fo awful, fo anxious a moment in the hiftory of mankind, never fo portentous a crifis of human affairs, as that on which the fenate of England now deliberates. It is no longer on fubordinate points of policy, on party queftions, on domeftic difputes, that they muft decide; but by the iffue of their councils, the fate of this country is to be irrevocably determined. With what emotions of virtuous anxiety, with what energy of refolution ought not the reprefentatives of the people to approach the exercife of their functions, fince every eye is upon them, and the part which they fhall act in the awful drama of this day; for the pen of hiftory fhall be fufpended, when fhe fhall hereafter be about to record a period fo eventful, and an occafion fo full of deftiny! They have told the people that the emergency of the common weal is fo great, as to call for every facrifice and exertion from the private citizen; therefore

fore the private citizen muſt naturally, in his turn, look to them for that diſplay of public wiſdom and virtue, by which alone the country can be ſaved. How have his expectations been anſwered? *That ſenate which is to cope with the councils of France, has ſeen three of its members ſecede; and not a man appears to take their place!!!* For no one in his ſenſes will pretend to ſay, that thoſe who carry on the farce of an oppoſition, are capable of ſupplying the loſs of ſuch a man as Mr. Fox. Surely if men, (as they too often do in the eyes of the world) perſonify opinions, Mr. Pitt can hardly wiſh that ſuch an opponent as Sir John Sinclair would be ſilent. I know that I ſhall be told, that this phænomenon is owing to the unanimity of that auguſt aſſembly: but is the occaſion on which they deliberate, ſuch as reaſonably to induce unanimity? *Are the people unanimous without doors?* And is it this tame, this puſillanimous principle of unanimity, that could beat down the tall aſpiring form of generous ambition, that could ſubdue "that laſt infirmity of noble minds," "by which fell the angels," "the glorious faults of gods" and godlike men, if it exiſted with all its attributes and energies of mind about it in the Britiſh ſenate, when it deliberates on the means of ſaving the common-wealth?

At leaſt the legiſlature of France, at no period of public diſtreſs and danger, exhibited a ſimilar example. Though her parties and ſyſtems have followed each other faſter than wave chaſes wave; though the

the

the emigrant race of politicians, the Conftitutionalifts of 1789, the Briffotines, the Mountaineers, the Royalifts of 1797, have fucceeded each other in authority and fate; yet does France difplay lefs wifdom or eloquence in her debates, lefs fagacity in the views of her policy, or lefs effect and vigour in the execution of them? If with my Lord Bacon we believe that man is but what he knoweth, and that knowledge is therefore power, may we not fear left at fome time or other, " the race fhould be to the fwift, and the battle to the ftrong."

I have now fubmitted to you my opinion of the ftate of the country. It is with you to determine, and act, as it fuits your judgment. One word, however, before I conclude, as to my own motives: for at a period of public anxiety and ferment, like the prefent, it is difficult fo to conduct yourfelf as not to be fubject to mifapprehenfion. I declare then, that I have addreffed thefe confiderations to you, not only from no feditious intention whatever, but from the deepeft anxiety for the fate of my country, and a greater intereft in the welfare of its propertied orders, than they may, perhaps give me credit for. It is not only becaufe I am a foe to revolution, but becaufe I would facrifice all and every thing of perfonal intereft to prevent it, that I have publifhed my opinions. And if that opinion is true, *what will it avail you that the law has declared truth to be a libel.* But that opinion is directly againft the reign of the people. Corrupt, ignorant,

ignorant, deluded—they are, alas! only capable of the dreadful energy of suicide. To trust the complicated affairs of a great empire, the decomposition of its whole social system, and the establishment of a new one, to their uninformed minds, and savage passions, would be worse than madness in any man; those only would do it, those half-witted politicians, whose minds distempered by disappointed vanity, and the dangerous possession, of a little learning, talk about Liberty, Equality, and the Rights of Man; whose only liberty is a ferocious indulgence of their passions; whose equality, is the dragging down their superiors to their own level; and whose notions of right, are a permission to commit wrong. Such men as these

> "Would bring mankind back to their woods
> "and caves,
> "And cry that all but savages are slaves."

It is to prevent their reign, that I call on you; on you, whose influence, whose education, whose habits of life should enable you to discern the cause of the evil, and to supply the remedy: to prevent your lying down to sleep, in the flattering but delusive security that "to morrow will be fair;" to prevent the continuance of a scene, which is the disgrace of this country, and the triumph of it's enemies; and which if it is not changed by timely reform, will be put an end to, by those terrible energies which nature

sometimes

sometimes calls up in the miseries and madness of mankind.

There is nothing so easy, and nothing more frequent than self deceit. Drowning wretches, it is said, will catch at straws; and those who are addicted to a darling error, are obliged to any friend who will furnish a defence of it: but the worst of this plausible philosophy is, that it's votaries generally *commit the action, and then hunt for the apology.* And where is the action which sophistry cannot palliate and recommend? So in political affairs, and particularly with respect to this country, all timely reform has been procrastinated or rejected, because mankind have been unable to make a virtuous sacrifice of their reigning habits or passions whilst a hope remained that the cruel necessity could be avoided. And they have endeavoured to delude themselves into the opinion, that they acted from principle. Hence have we seen elaborate treatises in favour of tyranny and corruption, from professed friends to the constitution and reverend ministers of religion. And hence at every successive period, at which the question of reform has been presented to the nation or it's Parliament, the danger of innovation, and the want of any specific remedy to the grievances complained of, have been reiterated. As to the first objection, let it be sufficient to remark with Mr. Burke that *to innovate is not to reform*; it will be quite sufficient to the wants of the people, if the country was restored to the " propriety " of thofe old and refpectable habits of life, of civil liberty and focial intercourfe, from which it has been " frighted :" if its government was brought back to thofe principles of public intereft, by which it was once fecured; if it's governors carried the virtues of an unblemifhed private life into the exercife of their public functions: and if the people, inftead of being an ignorant and corrupt rabble, the fubject of compaffion to their friends and derifion to their haters, were taught by the precept of their fuperiors to underftand what virtue and knowledge meant, and to admire and cultivate them by their example. And as to the other contemptible but hacknied objection, that it is eafy to detect error, and complain of evil, without fuggefting a remedy; are thofe that talk thus, ignorant *that no remedy was ever yet difcovered without a pre-exifting evil*: that falfe notions in fcience ftimulated the fublime faculties of a Newton to the difcovery of his immortal fyftem: that the unremedied infirmities of human nature have been the caufes of that improvement, to which the ftudies of anatomy and medicine have been brought: and that it is therefore equally reafonable, for the citizen of every ftate freely and loudly to complain of public difafter and grievance, fince thereby haply may be raifed up to her, fome mafter fpirit capable of redeeming the age he lives in, and of reftoring to his nation, like another Scipio, the peace and glory which fhe had loft. But even this fubterfuge re-

mains

mains not to the English public. Need I recal to your memories those illustrious names by which the page of our history is adorned: whose labours were devoted to the cultivation of those arts of peace by which the happiness and condition of mankind are extended and improved: of arts, more glorious than all the triumphs that war ever showered on the conqueror, or intrigue on the politician: the study and endeavour to render mankind, wiser, better, and therefore happier, than they were. It is to the truths which they taught, the discoveries which they made, and the measures they recommended, that I would call your attention. The evils that exist in our day in a greater degree, were not unknown, unfelt, undeplored, although they were unhappily unremedied in theirs. The corruption of the government, and people, the decay of public virtue, and the decline of national prosperity, called forth the zeal and energy, of the patriarchs of English liberty: of the Hampdens, the Sydneys and the Russells of former times: of the Somers and Godolphins: the St. Aubyns, Chathams, Camdens and Savilles of a later period; and of all the most distinguished public characters of our own. Of these it is true, all have been equally unfortunate: and one of these, Sir George Saville, recorded his opinion and despair of the state of the nation, by a solemn appeal to his constituents: let it not therefore be said by you, that you are without a guide: again and again has the path and the only path to salvation been pointed out to you, although you have been deaf to the voice of warning, and with the perverse ingratitude by which the public of most countries, but particularly of this have been distinguished, persecuted and reviled your real and generous friends, and branded with the stigmas of treason and rebellion those illustrious men whom an age of liberty and reason would have adored, and of whom the present "world is not worthy."

If the evils and dangers of your situation are really such as I have described them to be, you cannot therefore lay this "flattering unction" to your souls, that the means have not been pointed out, by which they can be remedied and averted. Those means consist simply in *national reform*. Not in the reform, that is supposed to be the watch-word of a political faction; not the œconomy of "cheese-parings and candle-ends;" not a reform in part and in detail, but in principle and system. First, are the manners of the people, corrupt; what is their source? The government. Therefore the government should have its abuses corrected. Has the public spirit and virtue of the nation declined; let those who are at the head of its classes and interests, begin the restoration of ancient patriotism, and a purer morality. And let it be remembered that this reform, like all other works of a similar nature, must begin in the efforts and examples of individuals. It is true that all this will exact from the public, what under the influence

of

of reigning habits, they will deem a difficult and painful sacrifice: viz. *that they will dare to be honest:* for prosperity has ever been the handmaid of virtue. The path therefore which you must tread, will I fear seem rugged and steep to the feet of luxury and selfishness; yet it is the path, which the most shining examples of human virtue have trodden before; and if it does not allure by the blandishments of pleasure and repose, still it conducts to the temples of honour, and the dwellings of peace.

O that mankind had adhered to the simple but delightful maxim of our religion, the sum and perfection of all our duties! To act by others, as we wish that they would act by us. What rivers of blood, what ages of misery would not have been spared the human race! Had you done thus, when you ought to have appealed to this moral test, for the regulation of your conduct, what would not have been the prosperity and happiness of this people, at the present hour. Had you done so, instead of offering up prayers that were a mockery of providence; instead of indulging in arrogant and foolish invective against jacobins and levellers, because you were righteous over much; instead of listening with delight to the homilies of your clergy, which were a *comment of war on the gospels of peace*; you would, by the spirit of a mild devotion and exemplary morality; by not hating and persecuting even those who hated and persecuted you; and by displaying the

excellence

excellence of your government, in the bleſſings of of order and peace, have proved the ſuperiority of your faith, your morality, and your conſtitution. But what has been your conduct? You have "kept the word of promiſe to the ear, and broke it to the hope." In 1792, when the country was flouriſhing in her people and reſources, you thought proper to raiſe the cry of war againſt the French, and of alarm againſt your fellow-citizens. How loud and ſolemn was the pledge of your zeal over conſtitutional dinners, and loyal bumpers! how active were its exertions! The ſyſtem of ſocial inquiſition, which you and your leader, Mr. Chairman Reeves, eſtabliſhed over the face of the country, ſpared neither the palace from its ſtate, nor the cottage from its inſignificance. Give me leave to tell you, that though you did this, as you profeſſed, to preſerve the Engliſh conſtitution, yet, by doing it, you did more to injure and overthrow it than all the harangues of Thelwall, or writings of Paine. Diſtruſt, revenge, intolerance, an odious diſtinction of intereſts between the higher and lower orders; an hatred of liberty on one part, a frantic licentiouſneſs on the other; a complacency towards ſlavery, oppoſed to a fanatical impatience of all government, have been the fruits of your wife aſſociations, of your pledge to ſupport the government with your lives and fortunes. For. in that ſtorm of conflicting paſſions, in the rage of oppoſite extremes, the genius of the Britiſh conſtitution was over-

whelmed

whelmed and vanquished. And do you now think that your persecuting spirit and frantic alarm, because it was armed with the thunders of the state, *has* secured the constitution from Jacobins and Levellers? Let the progressive increase of restraints on the liberty of popular discussion and meeting speak to this fact. You dare not trust the people. You know that they are not converted or satisfied, because they are silent: for you ought to know, that to increase burthen and grievance, is not the way to remove complaint and dissaffection; nor is it the happiest mode of retaining the affection and confidence of the people, to pledge your lives and fortunes to them for the support of the war, when your lives and fortunes were not wanted; and when they were, to abandon your pledge and your country at the same time, and, sheltering yourselves in a cowardly obscurity, leave the people to finish a contest as well as they can, in which they embarked *on your behalf alone*.

So much for your justice, your charity, your sincerity. One word more let me add on the score of policy before I take my leave of you, and I have done. If you were sincere in your alarm in 1792, and thought the pledge of your lives and fortunes necessary to preserve the government, what must be your fears, and what ought to be your exertions, in 1798? In 1792, the nation, from the blessings of peace, and the adoption of some prudent measures,

was

**IMAGE EVALUATION
TEST TARGET (MT-3)**

Photographic
Sciences
Corporation

23 WEST MAIN STREET
WEBSTER, N.Y. 14580
(716) 872-4503

was recovering faft from her former calamities. Public happinefs, at leaft, in thofe refpects, in which it is fenfibly felt by the people, had increafed and was increafing. The articles of life were cheap, the means of fubfiftence eafy, the public credit reftored, and its debt in a train of liquidation. In the midft of this fcene of growing profperity, there exifted a few vifionary enthufiafts, and a few turbulent fpirits, who were clamorous for a change; and who, with the energy of all rifing fects, were active in the propagation of their doctrines. But the little effect that they had produced on the public mind, is proved from the ftate of their numbers and refources, at the late trials for high treafon; and ftill more by the general, and even violent, expreffions of loyalty which your alarms and affociations produced throughout the country. In 1798 the fubject has been deprived of the effence of his political exiftence; whilft by the enormous expences of the war, and its baneful effects on induftry, he is at once commanded to pay a contribution, and robbed of all means of raifing it. Let me afk you then, whether thefe facts are not more dangerous illuftrations of the truth of levelling principles, the juftice of difcontent, and the neceffity of plans of innovation, than all that the labours of the London Corresponding Society could have afforded. Thefe are proofs unfortunately " fenfible to feeling as to fight." A reforming orator might harangue from a field pulpit for ever on liberty, truth, and mind, in the jargon

gon of a system absurd in itself, and not understood by its advocates themselves, and he would be heard without material danger, *because the people are not worked up to insurrection, without great and inveterate oppressions.* They will not lay aside their received prejudices and ordinary habits, without strong necessity. A demagogue, therefore, never yet has, and never will excite them to violence, by speculative truths and distant motives. But give him facts to reason with, and he is dangerously armed. Instead of talking of the Rights of Man, let him point to their starving families, state to them the price of provisions and labour; and insinuate that these are the results of their political system, and they will not only think but act with him. The people heed not remote consequences: *to relieve pain is the instinct of nature, and to relieve it by the speediest means.*

If therefore you are insensible to motives of an higher nature, let mere selfish policy prevail with you to lay aside this ruinous dishonesty. The die is not yet cast; although the balance trembles with your fate. The people have not yet renounced you: you are, even now, the children of one parent; the brethren of a common family. Let your reign be the reign of affection, not of fear; and there is nothing which kindness and benevolence may not do with the English people. You have, by your ruinous system, degraded, oppressed, and corrupted them; but there still remains about them so much moral sensibility, if not

not principle, that a little attention to their prefent wants would banifh all remembrance of former hardfhip and fuffering from their minds. If you dread the people, from their difcontents, is it not wife to remove the caufe of that alarm? If you are compelled to wage a war in which you want their affiftance, is it not reafonable that you, who are to reap the advantage of the victory, fhould endure the hazard of the conflict? If peace, however, is the pearl of price, if fuffering humanity and felf-prefervation invite you to put an end to the horrors of bloodfhed, fhould the paltry confiderations of a fugar or a fpice ifland prevent or delay the return of fo dear a bleffing? It is not only " vanity and crime," when the blood of man is fhed for other purpofes " than to redeem the blood of man;" but it is an abfurd impiety to fuppofe, that the Deity can profper a nation whofe conduct is governed by the motives of fo horrid and diabolical a policy: and if you really hope or wifh for the return of peace, do you believe that it ever will be obtained on a fecure footing, until you have folemnly renounced the principles on which the war was begun and continued; until you have difmiffed thofe men from power in whom *hoftility to France is a second nature?* Place yourfelves in the fituation of the French nation; remember what they have fuffered, what they might have expected, what they know and feel; and then fay whether, in your confciences, you fhould wifh or endure to receive even peace *from thofe*

*very*

*very hands that are yet streaming with the blood of your slaughtered fellow citizens!* Not until the memories of the French are obliterated, can they hear the name of Pitt without indignant frenzy; the whole nature of man must be reversed if they did: nor can he be the restorer of peace to the two nations; *for the destroying angel does not at the same time carry death and healing on his wings.*

And oh! above all things, divest yourselves, ere it is too late, of that false and treacherous security into which you are lulled by the apparent torpor of the people; it is neither content or patience. Alas! they do not feel the less keenly, because they dare not meet to pour out their indignant griefs on the bosoms of each other. But their "curses, although not loud, are deep;" if they are not published from the house-top, and on the highway, they are murmured from the gloom of dungeons and hovels. Their situation has so much physical suffering in it, that they must perforce both feel and think; and, whatever the verdict that they shall sooner or later return, may be, let it be recollected, that it will be the voice of Fate, which can neither be recalled or resisted.

From the Government I have no hope: they are infatuated. It is with them, as with all establishments, their misfortune and fault, to imagine that they can render themselves immortal; forgetting that they, in common with all works of time, must be subject to its influence; and that it is not given to any thing under the sun to be "incapable of perversion, and exempt from decay." Civil government is, or ought to be, the creature of circumstance; for it is a code of rules, adapted to the existing necessities and relations of a community. To perpetuate institutions when their end and reason are no more, argues therefore rather an irrational superstition, than a decent and honorable reverence.

The experience of your own lives must have taught you, gentlemen, that in human affairs *example is every thing*. It is so in public as well as in private Life. What volumes have been written on morality, whose contents are either unknown or forgotten! What laborious research has been expended on the theory of government, without having contributed to the liberty or happiness of the world! But when lived there a good man, who did not extend the blessings of his character beyond the mere circle of personal agency by the influence of his example; and when lived there a real patriot that did not become the polar star of the nation that was blessed with his existence? If then such things can be done by the example of one honest man; if sinking nations have been saved by the virtue of an individual citizen, what might not a community do, every member of which was impressed with the godlike imagination, that on his single effort the fate of his country depended? What is there in nature so impossible,

which

which the energy of such a people could not surmount?

It is to the saving influence of this sentiment, could it but become general amongst the people of England; and not to rhetorical artifice, to appeals to the passions, to diplomatic morals, or a scheme of political action conceived in a spirit of detail, that you can look for safety, or even for existence. You have trodden the path of dishonesty long enough, and to no purpose; try now then if better things may not be obtained by acting up to *the honest* in public as well as in private life. The science of politics you have been told, is an abstruse and entangled study. I will not positively assert, that it has been hitherto found so, from a vain endeavour to act right on wrong principles; but of thus much I am sure, that it is at least worth the experiment to the happiness of mankind, to try whether, by substituting plain dealing and speaking in the place of equivocation and fraud, the profound mysteries of government may not be resolved into simple truths, and its ways of vice and evil become those of pleasantness and peace.

If, however, you are determined to persevere in the old system; if, as formerly, you disclaim all compromise, all concession; if you are resolved to coerce, and not conciliate, and to think that those who are not with you are against you—only take care, lest you are taken at your words, and lest those who are not with you shall be against you; for you are fast

reducing

ducing this country to a choice of alternatives; and if that choice muſt be made, dreadful as it is, he would be the vileſt of cowards and ſlaves that does not ſay, if governments and privileged orders are juſt to the people, may they be eternal! but if they are not, let the people be juſt to themſelves; for governments and privileges may have an end, but the people ſhall live for ever.

FINIS.

www.ingramcontent.com/pod-product-compliance
Lightning Source LLC
Chambersburg PA
CBHW021948160426
43195CB00011B/1267